SNAP OUT OF IT!

Six Steps to Banishing Bad Habits, Addictions, and Negative Thoughts

Dr. Herbert S. Cohen

with Nancy R. M. Whitin

M. Evans and Company, Inc.
New York

M. Evans and Company, Inc.
216 East 49th Street
New York, New York 10017

ISBN 0-87131-896-2

Printed in the United States of America

9   8   7   6   5   4   3   2   1

CONTENTS

ACKNOWLEDGMENTS

Special thanks to:

My wife, Anita, whose help and inspiration were greatly appreciated.

My daughter, Lauren, for her enthusiasm.

Michael McGrail, who started it all.

Fred Dulaney, for his time and efforts.

This book is dedicated to my patients, from whom I have learned so much and whose stories I share here.

PREFACE

For over thirty years, I've counseled patients who have a variety of psychological problems, from simple stress to major depression. As a psychotherapist and marriage and family therapist I have worked with teenagers, singles, professionals, parents, families, and retired people. During that time, I have attempted many therapeutic techniques, from analytical to behavioral. Consistently I have found that rapid and dramatic changes are possible with the approach described here.

The three powerful techniques that I have combined into a single plan of action really work. Individually, each one is effective; but in combination, they have an even greater impact.

My goal in writing this book is to share this method with you. All I ask of you, the reader, is to approach the book in the step-by-step manner in which it is written.

Snap Out of It!

The success I have observed over the years by hundreds of patients has convinced me that the technique is easy and efficient. You can accomplish the change(s) you want to make in a short amount of time.

Once you overcome the normal difficulties most people experience in going through change, you'll discover a freeing up and a clarity of thought that will be yours forever.

INTRODUCTION

Susan lost twenty-five pounds, and she's kept it off for five years now.

Dean has stopped smoking. Now he's jogging without gasping for air.

Joseph no longer suffers anxiety at work, and he has been promoted to vice president.

Maggie no longer obsesses about her divorce. She's started to trust men again.

Though I personally can take some of the credit for these successes, what the above people had in common was a simple, but effective, technique and a *real plan*. A plan they could trust and rely upon. A plan that wasn't too complicated. It's the very same plan I will be teaching you in this book. This book will not overwhelm you. It is intended to be short, so that you will get to the end and succeed. My patients have pointed out to me that some self help books can be too complex, impractical, and confusing. Sometimes if a book is too complex, a reader becomes overwhelmed and puts it down in frustration. This leads to guilt for having failed to finish the book and implement its advice. The guilt then leads to an increase in the very problem behavior the reader originally wanted to stop. The dieter, for example, eats cookies to assuage the feeling of failure in controlling a weight problem.

It's not unusual to forget what you read at the beginning of a book by the time you get to the end. Sometimes you take away three to four "pointers" about how to improve your life for the better—but these three or four points don't make a plan and chances are if you don't practice them, you'll rarely use them.

It's also not surprising that your behavior, whether it be overeating or smoking, can actually be exacerbated by your inability to deal with a program described in a book. You may even become bored or impatient before you finish reading.

This was the case with Bob, a bright young engineer who was used to following very detailed instructions in his everyday work.

"I can stop smoking," he said. Well, it wasn't long before Bob, who was accustomed to working step-by-step to achieve a concrete goal on his job, was unable to follow the advice he was reading. He found himself focusing on so many things at once that he became mired down in trying to change everything, or at least thinking about all these things. He began to feel powerless in the face of having to correct almost everything about himself—otherwise there was the possibility that he would forever fail at his efforts to stop smoking.

The more Bob read and the more he tried to change *everything* about himself, the more frustrated and guilty he felt, to the point that his smoking increased to counteract his negative feelings. But each time he lit up a cigarette he had severe guilt feelings about failing to accomplish what that particular book had told him he could.

Jennifer, like Bob, tried to change everything about herself—her thinking, her emotions, her weight, her relationships—all at once. An impossible task! Not surprisingly, she

Snap Out of It!

became frustrated and angry at herself when she failed to accomplish what was advised in the prescribed plan she had chosen to follow. This led to more stress, more unhappiness, and more depression. "I'm a failure!" she wailed in session. "Why can't I turn my life around like the plan says? I'll never be liked, I'll always be fat, I'll never get ahead at work."

"Relax. You need to simplify, you need to set realistic goals, one at a time," I said.

That's when I gave Jennifer the band and told her to put it around her wrist.

"What's this for?" she asked. "You'll see," I said. "Just wear it this week."

"Well, that's easy," she replied.

"Actually, you could say it's a *snap*," I chuckled.

CHAPTER ONE
It's a Snap

The technique I'm about to teach you in this book is easy to grasp, and that's one reason I call it a "snap." The other reason is because you use the band to help you—"snapping" it as a reminder of your goals. You might laugh, but it's not a toy bracelet—it will be a powerful tool in your quest for change.

My patients particularly like the band because they can use it anywhere—at the office, at a party, at school. Some people even give their band a friendly nickname to personalize their "helpmate."

The band has been used for decades, even in settings as serious as alcohol and drug addiction clinics to break habits and change behavior. Indeed, I wasn't surprised to see it featured on the television show *ER*. But I was surprised when I realized that the band technique really has never been introduced to the general public.

I'm sure you've heard about tying a string around your finger to remember something. And if you've ever written yourself a note in order to remember to do something, then you're already on the way to learning the behavior modification technique I'll be teaching you. The band will be your method of "reminding" yourself what you really want to do. And what you really want to do, change or improve, is the reason why you're reading this book in the first place.

SELF-CONTROL?

One of the great truths I have found is that human beings can change. You may be thinking, "Easier said than done." After all, you may have tried before and failed.

It's true that change is difficult. Obviously we all have our limits, but we also have *unlimited* potential. Think about it. The word self-control implies that you *can* change your behavior. What has prevented your past success?

Recently I attended a seminar sponsored by Harvard

Medical School, conducted by Dr. Herbert Benson. The objective of the conference was to discuss research about the mind/body connection. The belief, based upon the findings of published studies, is that patients can empower themselves. Physicians are now paying attention to the connection between beliefs, emotions, and thoughts in the healing process.

An important book, *Change Your Brain, Change your Life*, written by Dr. Daniel G. Amen, has been published regarding the chemistry of the brain. Emotions, it has been found, can be described in chemical terms. Neurotransmitters, such as endorphins, have been identified as enhancing our feelings of well being. This isn't surprising. You know that your body chemistry is different when you're feeling depressed or sad than when you're feeling happy and elated.

This is knowledge that we can apply to actively participate in our change. We need to believe that self control is possible. We also need to address the thoughts and feelings that underlie our ability to get moving in the right direction.

When you believe that you can succeed, you recognize that you have choice. But choice is still difficult. Especially if it involves concentrating on breaking patterns that you

9

probably learned growing up—patterns that have often prevented you from achieving your goals.

We all need a practical, concrete way to begin to alter our behavior. We also know that change is easier when it isn't odious and when we experience small successes along the way. Therefore, I have purposely kept this book short and direct. The aim is to help you to move forward by keeping focused on a clear, basic plan.

You will find an approach that is interactive and fun. Because it is designed to yield fast results, you're less likely to lose your motivation.

You can succeed if you follow the steps, and if you use the Snap Out of It technique to change only one behavior at a time. For instance, if you want to stop smoking *and* stop thinking about your ex-husband, you need to apply this method to only one of these at a time. When you have stopped thinking about the ex-husband, then you can move on to the smoking problem—which could be as much as six months later!

In fact, it's important that you zero in on your goal. Pick a goal. One goal. Think about what you would like to change.

I can understand if you're skeptical. Perhaps you've

already tried to break an old habit before . . . or maybe many times before.

Here are some reasons why the technique works:

1. The basic steps are easy to grasp.

2. The theory behind the steps is easy to understand.

3. You can apply the technique anywhere, anytime.

4. It's easy to remember.

5. The band will serve as a constant reminder.

6. If you slip, you just start again.

"I wear the band at the office, out to dinner, everywhere," laughs Connie S. "Every time I look down and see it there on my arm, I remember to stand up straighter, smile, and look confident. It's been wonderful for my self esteem."

"After the band helped me to stop smoking, I got another one for my fourteen-year-old son who's constantly biting his nails," explained Joseph G. "And it worked. Every time he felt like biting his nails, he used the band technique."

If you're still skeptical, let me again assure you that my band technique is not frivolous. It is based on "thought stopping," a proven psychological procedure. It is combined with several powerful behavior modification methods that, when integrated, become even more effective in changing behavior. The systematic approach is consistent with cognitive behavioral psychology. It recognizes that the path to changing ourselves lies not only in what we do but in what we think.

These time-tested techniques include:

• *Thought-stopping*
This is a method adapted by Joseph Wolpe in 1958 as a method of breaking obsessive thinking patterns. Thought-stopping is used to break the ritual of holding on to thoughts related to an anxiety or fear. Thought-stopping is most effective at breaking the cycle of unproductive thinking.

• *Deep relaxation*
Deep relaxation focuses on relaxing your whole body

while letting go of obsessive thoughts. This type of relaxation clears away negative behavior and sets up the right environment for positive changes to be made. Methods of deep relaxation involve breathing, stretching, and imagery.

• *Positive self-talk*

Self-talk is another widely used psychological technique that teaches the patient to focus on what he or she is saying to him or herself. We all have our internal dialogues. The feedback we give ourselves in any situation is our self-talk. For instance, someone who is nervous about an upcoming event might start an internal dialogue that runs like this: "I hope nothing goes wrong. What will I do if I forget something? What if it rains? I'm sure if I call someone for help they will laugh at me." One of my chief aims as a therapist is to change my patients' negative and obsessive self talk into a positive, constructive dialogue.

CHAPTER TWO
Getting Started—
Thinking about
Your Goal

Your first step is to identify what *you* consider important to change. Typically problems fall in the areas of weight/diet, smoking, bad habits, relationships, work, finances, etc.

You picked up this book for a reason. You felt you wanted to improve part of your life. You may think you have a vague idea of what you want to change, but are having a difficult time focusing. If so, scan the subjects below to see if you identify your problem areas:

Snap Out of It!

- What is your relationship with your mate? Your children? Your parents? Friends?

- Do you need to change your habits? Smoking? Dieting? Drinking? Procrastinating?

- Do you want to change your feelings? Anger? Worry? Fear?

- Are you excessively apprehensive about the friends your children select?

- Do you constantly worry about crime? Being attacked or robbed? Do you recheck locked doors, windows, etc., to the point of distraction?

- Are you overly concerned about germs?

- Do you have difficulty making decisions?

- Are you overly worried about money?

- Do you worry about whether you are perfect?

- Do you often say to yourself, "I wish I could stop thinking about . . ."?

If you answer yes to the questions about worrying, you'll want to change your thinking as the first step in the process of change. Can you zero in on what thoughts are keeping you from enjoying life? If so, stopping an obsessive thought pattern may be the goal you want to achieve. This may be slightly more difficult to identify or nail down than a particular behavior, such as quitting smoking. Try answering the questions below.

CLARIFYING YOUR GOAL.

Try to crystallize your goal in your mind. Take the time to look at the Goal Questionnaire below. It is essential that you spend at least ten minutes thinking your objective through and considering the reasons behind it. Ask yourself, "What is the right goal for me?"

Snap Out of It!

GOAL QUESTIONNAIRE ONE

1. The behavior/habit I am changing is. . . . *Eating habits*

2. What is it that happens? *Overeat; wrong foods*

3. Where does it happen? *mostly at home*

4. When does it happen? *mostly at night*

5. How do I feel when it happens? *Rotten*

6. Why do I want to stop it from happening? *health mobility Quality of life*

7. Am I ready to stop it? *yes*

8. Am I prepared for the change in my life that may occur if it stops? *Accepting D - I can adjust*

9. Am I ready to believe in myself? *yes*

10. Am I committed to following the Snap Out of It technique? *yes*

CHAPTER THREE

Have You Chosen the Right Goal?

Make sure the goal you choose is your goal. It cannot be anyone else's. I can't tell you how many people come into my office lugging with them goals that have been dictated to them by their mothers, spouses, bosses, etc.

Daria showed up one day with her son Bronson, an adorable eight-year-old who fidgeted constantly. So, for several sessions I listened to Daria's thoughts on why Bronson couldn't stop fidgeting.

Bronson would succeed for a while, but eventually—though he told Daria that he wasn't—the teacher reported that Bronson was indeed fidgeting at school. The more Bronson knew he was disappointing and deceiving his mother, the more guilty he felt, exacerbating his need to fidget.

The pressure of having a goal that was his mother's goal was too much for him.

Finally I leaned forward and asked Bronson, "Do you want to stop fidgeting?"

"Oh, yes." he nodded.

"Why?" I pressed.

"Because my mother wants me to. She says I look funny and that I would do better in school if I stopped."

"But, Bronson," I pursued, "do *you* want to stop fidgeting?"

Bronson looked very confused. He stared at me and then looked at his mother. It was obviously not something he had thought about.

"You, Bronson, do you want to stop fidgeting?" I asked again.

And then he smiled and answered softly, "Yes."

"Why?"

"If I didn't fidget, my friends would stop laughing at me," he said as a tear started to roll down one cheek.

That's when I knew that Bronson could be motivated. With a very "cool" band to wear, Bronson could feel he was in charge and he did not have to use his energy to resist his mother. He could instead channel his energy constructively because now he wanted to stop fidgeting for himself.

There's a pattern that people get into when they are trying to achieve a goal for someone else. It's a pattern that develops when they slip up. The bad behavior becomes aggravated by guilt-induced anxiety. There's a built-in mechanism that resists being controlled. It's almost as strong as the need to survive physically. Emotional survival is a very powerful drive. You see it in two-year-old children who are beginning to separate from the parent. Their oppositional stage (the terrible twos) is quite normal, as is a certain amount of adolescent rebellion.

I believe we are genetically predisposed to emotionally prepare ourselves to become independent from the parent. However, this tendency sometimes dominates us in reacting to an overbearing authority figure. Instead of going through normal stages of being emancipated, we are instead taken over by our need to resist. Assignments from school, diets, exercise, following orders from others or even from ourselves, all become directives that are resisted in a knee-jerk fashion. When this occurs as a pattern, it becomes self-defeating. Psychotherapists' offices are filled with people who are dominated by habits that they can't seem to control. Hence, much of psychotherapy is focused on modifying or working through habits that we might have needed at one time for emotional survival but are no longer necessary and are, in fact, counterproductive.

Here's how the patterns develop:

1. You promise a parent or spouse that you will try to change something.

2. You slip up: It could be a small temporary failure, but it usually leads to—

3. The cover up: Not wishing to disappoint a parent or spouse, you pretend you are still on target.

4. But now you have more reasons to feel guilty because you are being deceptive and you feel like a failure.

5. You now feel depression and anger, often the result

of guilt. You may be angry at yourself or at the person you feel you have disappointed.

6. You are then feeling so bad that you regress and fall back on the bad behavior in an attempt to make yourself feel better again.

When you are doing something for yourself, many of these counterproductive feelings are eliminated. If you don't feel you are doing something just to make someone else happy, you can stop pretending and deceiving, thus eliminating much of the guilt and anger.

Here's a conversation you can *avoid*:

Daria: Bronson, have you been fidgeting at school?
Bronson: No, Mom.
Daria: I heard from the teacher that you were.
Bronson: I'm sorry.

By choosing his own goal, Bronson need answer only to himself. He can proceed at the pace he chooses.

When you set a sight for yourself—a direction in which

you want to go—you are changing a self-expectation. There is now a demand on you to change. This has to be yours, not somebody else's. When you accept the fact that you are changing for yourself, then you can succeed.

• • •

Ruth complained that she wasn't able to lose weight. It wasn't her fault. No matter how often she tried, she always failed. "I want to do this for my husband and children. It's important that I please them. They say that they are embarrassed by me," she cried. "But I can't seem to change my situation."

Ruth's efforts failed because she was unconsciously resisting the pressure. She yearned to be accepted for who she was, not for how she looked. She actually resented that these expectations were being imposed on her. It wasn't until she came to want this goal for herself that she was able to lose weight and keep it off permanently.

Start with one simple and definable goal.

Not only must your goal be yours, but it must be simple.

Step 1: Your Goal

That's why I asked you to spend time thinking about your goal. It may seem elementary, but I can't tell you how many people fail because they hinge their feelings of success on too many factors. Their goal becomes too complicated and unattainable, and the inevitable frustration leads to guilt, anger, and failure. Here's an example.

Ted came in to my office one day and announced he was going to change.

"I'm going to be a healthier person," he said.

"How will you do that?" I asked.

"I'm going to stop eating junk foods. I'm going to run four times a week. And I'm going to stop drinking so much at parties."

"Wow, that would be a lot to accomplish all at once," I pointed out. "In fact it may be too much. Why don't you start with one goal? Say cutting out junk foods. Once you feel comfortable that you've succeeded in changing your eating habits, you can move on to the running part—maybe even three months from now."

Ted had to agree that it would indeed be easier to concentrate on the junk food habit without hinging its success or failure on the running program.

Snap Out of It!

I hope I have convinced you of the importance of picking a single goal. Once again, I can't stress enough that the goal you pick should be *your* goal and it needs to be a realistic goal.

Sean came into my office and announced that he wanted to stop smoking—it was his only problem. But it wasn't; I could readily see that he really needed to control his anxiety before he could stop smoking. After a few sessions I gave him the band to use in helping him to overcome his anxiety.

"I use this every time I want a cigarette, right?" he asked.

"No," I replied. "I just want you to snap the band every time you feel anxious."

"Can I still have the cigarette?"

"Yes, for now." I answered. "Because first I want you to get in touch with how you feel when you start to crave a cigarette. And next week we'll start learning how to change your smoking habit by reducing your feelings of anxiety."

"Are we going to drag in a whole lot of stuff—everything about my childhood and parents?" Sean asked.

"No. We're going to make it simple and tackle it head-on with behavior modification," I replied.

If Sean had chosen to work only on smoking, he may have

failed. But once he used the band to combat his anxiety, he was able to stop smoking for good.

So ask yourself, "Do I really want to lose weight? Or is it that I focus on my weight when I get angry at myself at work?" Or ask yourself, "Do I want to stop smoking first? Or is my fear of being rejected at the root of many of my bad habits?"

These are very difficult questions to answer on your own. Reexamine your answers to Goal Questionnaire One. Your self-examination lays the groundwork upon which change will occur.

Once you have picked a goal, I want you to answer Goal Questionnaire Two. Take some time to answer the questions about your goal and then pick one and only one goal you want to attain. It may be that you want to stop smoking or overeating. Or you may want to address something such as anxiety or your anger. Maybe you just got divorced and you want to stop obsessing about your ex.

I suggest that you find a comfortable spot, where you can be alone to answer these questions. If it's not possible to find that place or time today, then map out some time for yourself tomorrow or the next day. It is essential that you take the

Snap Out of It!

time to know your goal, be comfortable with your goal, and be fully committed to your goal.

GOAL QUESTIONNAIRE TWO

The goal I will be working on is: _wt Loss_ .
 (Make sure this goal is clear to you.)

1. Is this goal a goal I have chosen for myself? _yes_

2. Is it a goal to which I am totally committed? _yes_

3. How will I feel if I succeed? How will I be better? _Energy Activity_

4. Have I tried to accomplish the goal before? _yes_

5. If so, do I know why I failed in the past? _somewhat_

6. How are circumstances different with this attempt? _Doing it for me_

Staying on toochul my goals

7. Am I more committed than I was in previous attempts to change? How so?

more Positive

28

8. How will others react if I succeed? *PRAISE* *Resistance*

9. Is my goal simple and uncomplicated? *yes*

10. Is this the right time to start? Am I *ready* to start now? *yes*

11. List the pros of your goal to change.
    a. *Health*
    b. *Energy*
    c. *More Active*
    d. *Quality life, Friends*

12. List any cons that may result from your change.
    a. *people won't understand*
    b. *they'll treat me different*
    c. *I'll have to meet new friends*
    d. *I'm scared of ∆*

13. What friends or relatives may resist my attempts to change? *Mom, Jane, Gloria, Paul*

• • •

While you are in the process of thinking about a goal and making a commitment to change, I want to take a moment to

Snap Out of It!

talk about "change." As part of your commitment to change you should think about the following:

- Change is never easy. It is often very difficult. Don't expect instant success. Be persistent.

- You will need to be honest with yourself. You may have to admit that you have weaknesses that controlled you in the past.

- Change can mean you and others will look at who you are differently. In fact, some people may get angry that you are improving and they aren't. If you are losing weight, they may become jealous of you. You may have to change your idea of who you are, too. If you have lost weight, you may need to start thinking of yourself differently, as a slim, healthy, attractive person with a lot to offer.

- To change you need to follow a specific course of action. This you have chosen to do with my book, which will guide you along to success.

30

- Be happy with small successes on your route to change. Don't expect to succeed immediately. Accept small set backs, and don't give up.

Once you have picked a goal, I want you to do two more things:

1. Stop reading this book and put it aside for one to two days. Good places to keep it are on the night table, in your briefcase, or on the kitchen table. Just make sure you don't put it someplace where you'll forget about it.

2. Think about the goal you chose for one to two days. Be sure that after a day or two, you still feel comfortable with your goal. You'll know you've chosen the right goal if you're feeling especially positive about proceeding. Do not rush into a goal. If you need more information, ask for advice, reconsider, but be sure you are selecting a goal that inspires *you* to succeed.

• • •

Remember: The goal should be your goal. The goal should be uncomplicated.

Snap Out of It!

Your Journal

Use this space to keep a daily record of your feelings about the choice of your goal. Jot down any thoughts that occur to you about past efforts to change. What were your strengths and weaknesses? Write down anything that comes to you about your feelings.

• • •

_____

_____

_____

_____

_____

_____

_____

_____

_____

_____

_____

_____

_____

_____

_____

_____

_____

_____

_____

_____

_____

_____

_____

_____

_____

CHAPTER FOUR
One Step at a Time

Now that you have picked *one* goal to work on, I want you to proceed slowly. We're going to work on one phase at a time. Just think of it as an athlete would think of a goal. If you were an ice skater and you were going to learn a triple toe-loop you would start by learning *one* toe loop, right? It only makes sense.

If it were up to you to teach someone to drive, what would you do for a first lesson? If you cared about your own life, you'd go to an empty parking lot, not I-95 at rush hour! And you'd probably return to that parking lot a couple of times before venturing down a neighborhood street.

Remember, you've been a certain way for a long time. You've got to gradually establish a new process, a new

Snap Out of It!

behavior. *You* may want to change, but your head and body may resist.

That is why I don't want you to read this book all the way through at first. Later I will ask you to stop reading and practice what you have learned before proceeding or jumping ahead.

When you overload your home electrical wiring by running the washer, dryer, dishwasher, and television at the same time, and then turn on the vacuum cleaner—all of a sudden the circuits blow. Similar things may happen with your computer. If you have too many programs open at one time, the computer will "crash."

And I can safely predict, from all my personal and professional experience, that if you have too many goal "programs" running at the same time you too will "crash." This is why I want you to go slowly. Once you have mastered each step of the technique, you will process that step without effort and be able to go to the next step without overburdening your "system" and short-circuiting.

I'll illustrate this point.

Ralph was trying to improve his relationship with his wife. Sharon was ready to divorce him if he didn't change. He rarely communicated with her, was never affectionate, made sarcastic remarks to her, and often raised his voice at her when he came home angry from work. He was the same way with their children. Ralph went to one therapist who told him he needed to change all these bad behaviors at once—in other words, transform himself overnight. He came home and tried talking about the news, and then he tried hugging Sharon, and then he pitched in and helped with the housework—all in the same two hours. Ralph overloaded; he crashed. He felt so alien to himself that he ended up exploding.

The pressure to succeed was just so extreme that he buckled and did just what he hoped he wouldn't—he yelled at Sharon, who understandably responded by leaving the house and taking off in her car.

The marriage was now on the point of collapse. Sharon had moved in with her sister when Ralph came to see me.

"I can't change," Ralph lamented. "I love her so much, but I don't know how to be different. I really want to be. I know I can be a pain in the butt."

"You *can* do it," I said. "But you need to go slower."

"Sharon will leave," he moaned.

"No, Ralph." I said. "If you take it one step at a time, one baby step at a time, you'll succeed with each little step. And every triumph will be an encouragement to yourself and to Sharon. She will come to trust you a little more each time. You'll be building confidence in yourself and in Sharon. As you master each step, it will be easier for you to go on to the next without sliding back, because that step will become almost second nature."

Ralph brightened. "So, you think that if I only try communicating with Sharon over a period of several weeks, she'll be encouraged enough to be patient for a little bit longer?"

"And maybe Ralph, just maybe," I said, "chatting with Sharon will become a natural activity that you no longer have to practice."

"Yes, yes," Ralph mused. "And once it's second nature, I can move on to giving her more affection."

"With each success you'll be inspired to proceed further," I told him. "It's the frustration that you feel when you try to do it all at once—the frustration makes you angry, and you blow up."

I paused and waited for my point to sink in, then continued. "Ralph, you need to approach the problem rationally.

Step 2: The Band

For instance, how would I teach someone to swim if he was afraid of the water? First I'd have him stand in it and get used to the water. Then maybe the next time I'd have him stick his head under water and. . . ."

"Wow!" Ralph broke in. He was hopeful and happy now. He had a plan, a plan that moved from one step to the next. In his mind it was a plan that could work, because he only had to do it one step at a time. After he had completed one step he could move on to the next, and Sharon would be partially pleased at each step. Her trust would build as he proceeded.

This is the sort of plan I want you to follow as you read this book, which is why you shouldn't read this book all at once. Trust me, you would not remember everything—you would overload, stress-out, and crash. And, in frustration, you would stop trying altogether and you might automatically label yourself a failure, which could aggravate your bad habits.

I want you to put my book down, practice what you have read, and then move on to the next step once you feel comfortable—and, most important—confident.

Which is what Ralph did. Ralph started using the band and working on communicating with Sharon. He didn't worry about hugs, or chores, or anything but communicating. He told her about his day, what he was thinking, his plans, etc. But with the band technique targeted directly on one goal at a time, Ralph was able to progress and feel confident.

And the more Ralph progressed, the better he felt. Ralph was happier because he was succeeding. After all no one likes to fail. So with success came happiness, which all leads to the projection of a new Ralph, a Ralph that Sharon has found to be to her liking.

With my recommendation, Ralph didn't start using his band to achieve his next goal for a good three to six months. By then, communicating had become second nature to him, and he was ready to start working on his next goal.

● ● ●

Here is an overview of your personal plan to success with the Snap Out of It band. In general, these are the steps and the time-frame in which you must operate in order to succeed using my program. If, while learning the technique, you ever have the desire to rush ahead or change the program you should turn back to this plan page and read the steps along with the time plan.

Step 2: The Band

YOUR PLAN: STICK TO THIS SCHEDULE

STEP	TIME
1. Read chapters 2 and 3; pick a goal	1 to 2 days
2. Read chapters 4 and 5; wear the band	3 days minimum
3. Read chapter 6; learn the Snap and Stop	3 days minimum
4. Read chapter 7; master deep relaxation	3 days to 2 weeks
5. Read chapter 8; start talking to yourself	2 weeks
6. Read chapter 9; put it all together	2 weeks
7. Maintenance	ongoing

Snap Out of It!

THINGS TO REMEMBER WHILE FOLLOWING THE PLAN

1. *Stick to the plan.*

2. *Progress at the prescribed speed.* For instance, do not pick a goal in 10 minutes. Think about it for a day or two.

3. *Be patient with yourself.* If you falter and slip up, just repeat the step until you get it right.

4. *Move through the plan at a reasonable rate.* If you leave too much space between mastering the steps, you will lose the momentum and motivation that ties the strategy all together.

5. *Stick with only one goal throughout the plan.* If you add goals, you will be overloaded.

6. *Keep a journal.* Keeping a diary or journal of your progress will help to keep you motivated and on target. I have provided pages so you can make your entries right in the book. By using the book as a journal as you proceed through the program, you will develop a stronger bond with the technique, and your commitment to your goal to change will be stronger and more personal.

Step 2: The Band

"Why should I have to follow this plan?" asked Randy, who wanted to stop exploding and shouting at people. It was just like Randy to challenge any "rules." He considered himself to be smarter than average and a renegade.

So I took a deep breath and explained. "Randy, you want to proceed slowly and deliberately. This is not instant magic. Remember, Randy, you've been exploding at your coworkers and family for just about half your life. It's not unreasonable to think that you can't change. But give the band a try. If you invest a little bit of time and patience, the result will be success."

"Randy," I continued, "you may really *want* to change, but your head and your gut will resist the change because they're comfortable with the way you have always been. The reason you haven't been successful in the past is because you were accustomed to following what was familiar."

We all have two powerful forces operating on us all the time: our head and our feelings. Some people follow their head in a logical manner, but lack feelings. Psychologists call them neurotically constricted. They are the kind of people who seem rational, logical, and even very mature; however, they lack warmth and empathy.

Snap Out of It!

The opposite type of people are guided by their emotions to an extreme. They follow the 'If it feels good, do it' philosophy. They seem to feel that their emotions know best. It's like relying on your dog to let you know when he's had enough to eat.

But we can't always trust our emotions. They tend to perpetuate what feels familiar regardless of the effect the behavior has on us, whether good or bad. Unbridled emotions are what psychologists call immediate impulse gratification: in other words, giving in to the emotion, regardless of the consequences. Underachievers—people with little inner discipline—fall into this category. They might say, "I'm lazy. That's why I can't follow a diet, or get into an exercise regime." In order to achieve your desired goal, you need to get in touch with your feelings, and then determine on a rational, logical level what triggers your bad habit.

"This is like war, Randy." I told him. "There's a contest going on between you and the other you. And I promise that the new Randy can win this contest if you have a strategy. After all, even General Patton had to follow a strategy to win his battle. And the battle you'll be fighting will be all the more difficult because the 'old soldier' in you won't die, he'll keep reappearing and reappearing until he slowly fades away. You'll need a plan to keep from surrendering to such a persistent foe. Remember, this foe—the 'other you'—knows you very well. The 'other you' knows where your weaknesses lie. The 'other you' can kidnap the real you in order to get what he wants, whether it's food, cigarettes, alcohol, whatever. You'll need to be strong to resist, and this strategy gives you a means to overcome the foe."

I leaned over and slipped the band onto Randy's wrist. "This band will help. Consider it a tool."

"So Doctor," he asked, "what does the strategy say I should do first?"

• • •

Do not read any further in this book until you have thought about your goal for a least a full day. Solidify your commitment. Keep your journal on page 32.

• • •

See you in a day or two!

45

CHAPTER FIVE
The Band

Read this chapter as part of Step 2.

You've picked your goal, and you're feeling good about proceeding. You feel confident because the goal is *your* goal and it's a simple, straightforward goal.

Now it's time for the fun part. You're ready to start wearing the band. That's it. Just slip it on. If you're right-handed, place it on your left wrist, and vice versa.

I want you to get comfortable with just wearing the band for the next three days. I want you to bond with your Snap Out of It band. Consider it your friend, your partner in change, and give it a name if you like.

Some of my patients have chosen names such as Buzz, Faith, Bob, Mozart . . . they all have a reason behind the name. This may sound silly right now, but read on, and I think you'll begin to understand.

Your band will go everywhere with you. It won't let you forget about what you hope to do. You'll be able to keep the band with you as a reminder of your goal.

If you're at a party, the band is right there with you silently reminding you about your goal to watch your diet. It will be up to you if you let the band become your friend. Unlike a nagging spouse, it will be hard to get annoyed with the band. Your band will not say, "Hey, you're on a diet." The band will remind you to say to yourself, "I'm on a diet."

It's a subtle difference, but it's a big one. It's all about deciding and doing something for *yourself*. But, at the same time, it's about keeping that goal in front of you. "Keeping your eyes on the prize," so to speak. (This concept is so simple that it works exceptionally well for children with problems. How many times does a child say, "I forgot" when it comes to changing behavior? With the band you explain to the child, "The band is your friend and it will help you to remember your goal." Tell your son or daughter that you won't be reminding them over and over again. They can look for support from their buddy, the band. No more nagging. No more disappointing Mom.)

48

Step 2: The Band

Over the next three days as you get to know your band, wear it constantly. Each time you look at the band I want you to think, "This time it will work." I'm warning you that some people who embark on the Snap Out of It technique will look down at the band and think, "This won't work. I couldn't change before. Why should this work?"

Try your very best not to get caught up in this self-fulfilling prophesy. I will get into "self talk" later as a tool to combat this sort of negative thinking.

• • •

Martha came into my office complaining of headaches. She admitted that when I gave her the band, she thought to herself, "This won't work either." It doesn't take a genius to realize that the band couldn't work for Martha until she had changed her attitude.

On the other hand, we're all familiar with the placebo affect. If someone believes that a pill will work, it does. So you must keep negativity and skepticism out of your mind when you look at the band. When you look at the Snap Out of It band on your wrist I want you to smile and think "It's going to work. And when I accomplish my goal, I'll be a happier person."

Snap Out of It!

If someone asks you why you are wearing the band, you might answer, "It's to remind me to do something" or "To help me stop smoking" or "I just like it, I'm starting a new fad."

But be prepared—you may meet some surprising hostility when you mention your new goal to your friends or relatives. In fact, people may be downright mean: "Right; you're going to stop smoking, like you did twenty times before."

•   •   •

Keith complained that every time he announced that he was going to stop drinking, his friends would laugh at him. "I failed in all my other attempts, so they thought nothing of passing me a beer when they knew I was trying to quit," he moaned.

"Do you understand that your friends were threatened by your goal?" I asked.

"Why would they be threatened if I stop?" Keith asked. "They can still drink."

"It's both simple and complicated at the same time, Keith." I told him. "You see, your change makes them feel uncomfortable because they themselves may be in conflict about drinking—or other behaviors, for that matter. If you succeed in meeting *your* goals, and they haven't met whatever goals they might have, it makes them feel like more of a failure. And there's also fear. The fear of change is powerful. Your friend Bob might be subconsciously thinking, 'Hey if Keith stops drinking, we won't be able to have fun together. What if the other guys stop, too? What will I do on a Saturday night?'"

Keith pondered for a few moments, then said, "So they could be thinking that if I change, something in their world will change, and they won't have any control over it."

"You got it. In a nutshell, people feel threatened by change; it makes them uneasy. They're afraid of how they may be affected. If *you* change, *they* have to make an adjustment."

"So how do I deal with them?"

"My advice to you is to reassure anyone who seems threatened by your goal. For instance, your response to Bob could be, 'Bob, just think, if I stop drinking, you won't have to worry about who's going to be the designated driver.'"

"Well, there's a plus," Keith admitted.

• • •

Be prepared for hostility, but don't take offense. The change you make will be for the positive. You just need to reassure your friends and relatives that you'll still be "you," so to speak.

• • •

It was Cathy who said, "I don't need a band. I *know* I shouldn't be eating cookies."

"It's true Cathy." I agreed. "You know you shouldn't be eating cookies right now. But, when you're under stress, will you conveniently 'forget' about your wish to lose weight?"

• • •

When you're stressed, you automatically seek instant relief from your old standby, whether it be cookies, cigarettes, alcohol, or anger and withdrawal. And then, pow— goals go out the window. This is where the band is particularly handy , in the midst of a crisis. Maybe your boss just put you down. You're stressed, you reach for a cigarette and there is the band, reminding you that despite your agitated feelings, you have a goal—a goal you want to accomplish in spite of your "idiot" boss.

The band is a firm reminder of the target you're focused on. Your goal is visceral, it's real—it's not just some abstract thought you try to hold on to in your head. It's a real goal. Look at the band, and you know it's there for a reason; you put it there for a purpose.

The band concept is not new; it's been in use for quite a while. First developed in the 1950s, it is still used to help people cope with stressors in their lives. It has been applied to treating symptoms as simple as test anxiety to controlling obsessive behavior. As mentioned earlier, the band method was even featured in a 1997 episode of the television program *ER*.

As simple as it may seem, it works. It's user friendly, simple enough for a child to operate, won't break down, and is machine-washable.

The band doesn't plug into a wall socket, but it does run on your attitude.

For those who want to simplify their lives, the band is a breath of fresh air.

● ● ●

Let's go back to Cathy. She knows she shouldn't eat cookies, but she eats them if something starts to bother her. As soon as she falls behind at work, she starts with the sweets.

Snap Out of It!

"I guess I forget temporarily." She said. "I'm all caught up in the stress of the moment and, in that moment, taking care of the immediate stress seems more important than any long-term goals. So I run for the cookies."

"And how do you feel after you eat the cookies in response to the work stress of the moment?" I asked.

"I feel good for about fifteen minutes..." she admitted. "And then I feel really bad after I realize that I just sacrificed a long term goal and a previous week's worth of dedicated dieting."

"That's because you were caught up in the anxiety of the moment," I told her. "You were seeking instant relief from the stress at hand, and that's only natural. And this is where the Snap Out of It band helps. The band serves as a friendly reminder that you have a precious goal you really want to keep. It helps you focus on the big picture, the long term, and release yourself from the stress of the moment."

• • •

As I told Cathy, I want you to wear the band for several days before you proceed to Step 3, as described in the next chapter. Again, put this book down in an obvious spot and wear the band. In fact, the band will serve as a reminder that you need to continue with the book and the technique if you want to make the change you desire.

Some patients want to know if it's okay to "snap" the band during these first several days. I prefer that you do not. Snapping will be described in the next chapter.

You can wear the band when you sleep, exercise, or shower. Or take it off and place it with your watch so you won't forget it. You should consider your band a "fun" accessory that is also a helpmate—a best friend, of sorts.

• • •

Remember: Stick to the plan. And only proceed at the recommended speed.

• • •

You have now finished:

• Step 1: Choosing your goal

• Step 2: Adjusting to your band

Snap Out of It!

Your Journal

As you spend the next three days wearing the band, return to this space each night to note any reactions or feelings you had about the band, the program or the goal you have chosen. Do you understand the first part of this program? Are you committed to proceed? Remind yourself why you want to succeed as you write your daily thoughts.

• • •

_____

_____

_____

_____

_____

_____

_____

_____

Step 2: The Band

_____

_____

_____

_____

_____

_____

_____

_____

_____

_____

_____

_____

_____

_____

_____

_____

CHAPTER SIX
Snapping and Stopping

Read this chapter as part of Step 3.

Step 3, called Snap and Stop, is a little more complicated than the previous exercises, but you will master it easily if you are patient with yourself. I'm recommending that once you read this chapter (reread it if you must), you practice this technique for at least three days. If you need to take a few additional days don't worry.

Here, in Step 3 you finally get to snap. But you won't be snapping the band randomly. If snapping the band becomes a nervous habit, you will destroy the whole reason for wearing the band. Yes, it is true you are wearing the band as a reminder, but it will now turn into an interactive reminder. When you snap the band, you will be snapping it for a specific purpose.

Snap Out of It!

Snapping the band means stop!

Before I explain the procedure in specific detail, I'll use an example from one of my cases.

Bob was seeing me at the request of his wife, who wanted a divorce. Bob knew the only way to save his marriage was to stop losing his temper at home with his wife and children. Bob, I decided, was a perfect candidate for the band. He was highly motivated, and he had a goal that he both wanted and needed to achieve.

"This *band* is going to help me? How?" Bob asked with anger in his voice.

"Stay calm and listen to me, "I said "and I will explain how it will start to help you in the Snap Out of It technique. The purpose of the band will be to stop you in your tracks.

"Every time you look down and see that band on your wrist, Bob, I want you to remind yourself of your goal to control your anger. And then, when you are in a situation at home and you feel yourself getting angry, I want you to snap the band and think, 'stop.'"

"Is it like a time-out?"

"Yes, you could call it that. Actually you can think or say out loud, 'Stop,' 'No,' or even 'I can do it.' This action will be a conscious choice on your part, an acknowledgment of your goal as you begin to stop the bad behavior."

"I see. By snapping the band I remind myself that I don't want to get angry, and by thinking, 'Stop,' I have a chance to reconsider my actions in light of my goal," Bob theorized.

I was delighted with Bob's precise rephrasing of the Snap and Stop concept. I hadn't really thought about the word "reconsider" before. And it's a very good term with regards to Snap and Stop because this step does give you time to *reconsider* your actions. It reminds you of your goals and offers you a chance to stop what you were about to do wrong.

So now that you have the big picture, I will walk you step by step through learning to Snap and Stop.

First, take a minute here to refresh your memory about the previous two techniques you have learned:

1. You have chosen your goal, and you are committed to seeing it work.

2. You have worn the band for at least three days in order to get accustomed to it.

Snap Out of It!

Now we'll start on the third part of the technique, Snap and Stop.

SNAP AND STOP

First, be aware of your thoughts and goals. Next, when you feel you are about to misbehave, look at your band to remind yourself of your goal. Then, snap the band and think or say "Stop."

Let me give you some specific examples. Let's start with dieting.

You're at a friend's house for dinner, and you're tempted to have a second helping of the delicious mashed potatoes.

In the back of your mind, something is nagging at you: eating more potatoes would sabotage your goal. (This is the first Snap and Stop step: be aware of your thoughts and goals.)

Look at your band to reinforce your knowledge that you have indeed made a promise to stay on a diet.

Then, snap the band and think, "Stop!"

If you want to stop worrying, the technique is similar. Let's say your children are going to the beach with their friends and their friend's parents. There's no need to worry.

You can't get anything done at work, you realize you are needlessly and obsessively worrying about your children; your friends are extremely responsible people. (The first step: be aware of your thoughts and goals.)

Look at your band to remind yourself of your goal to stop worrying constantly.

Snap the band and say, "Stop!" Remind yourself you are foolishly worrying in this case.

Keep practicing this technique for at least three days. If you are not using the Snap and Stop step consistently after three days, you should keep practicing for up to two weeks. If you slip up, it's okay. Don't give up. You haven't slipped back really. Just remember to keep snapping the band and saying, "No."

•   •   •

Remember: Be patient with yourself.

•   •   •

Of course I'm not implying that just by saying "No" or "Stop," you will be able to change your behavior in a week.

Snap Out of It!

This is just the third easy step of the six steps you will combine in the Snap Out of It technique. Most likely just by snapping the band and saying "Stop" or "No," you will stop temporarily, now and then. You will need to add the additional steps to make a real change in your behavior.

Snap and Stop is not a radical idea. It is based on the commonly practiced psychological technique called thought stopping. I want to reassure you that Snap and Stop is not hocus-pocus.

In *Thoughts and Feelings: The Art of Cognitive Stress Intervention* by McKay, Davis, and Fanning, the technique is described as "Thought interruption and thought substitution. At the first hint of a habitual thought that you know leads to unpleasant emotions you interrupt the thought by sub- vocalizing the word 'stop' or by using some other interrupting technique. . . . Thought interruption acts as a 'punishment' or distracting tactic."

And, as they also note, the idea of "stopping" was first introduced in Bain's 1928 book *Thought Control in Everyday Life*. Joseph Wolpe and others in the 1950s employed Bain's technique to deal with obsessive or phobic thoughts.

Step 3: Snap and Stop

Snapping a band around your wrist while shouting "No" is also not an original idea. Edna Foa and Barbara Rothbaum write about this technique in their book *Treating the Trauma of Rape*: "She should snap the rubber band lightly while silently shouting *stop*. This action often helps jolt the thought away, much as the startling effect of shouting *stop!* does. If she likes using it, suggest that she can wear the rubber band always, making sure it isn't too tight."

There are several theoretical analyses of why thought-stopping works. These are based on a conditioning model. The idea is that we can change old behaviors by making new connections. Your band may be an escape from unwanted thoughts. The band acts to distract you from the behavior you don't want and to change your direction. It also acts as a physical reminder—a kind of shock, or a little "ouch," that helps you to resist the old habit.

Okay, now you're ready to practice "Snap and Stop" for at least three days. If you're not an "expert" after three days, take more time. If you haven't perfected this step in two weeks, you either aren't focusing or you're not committed to meeting your goal, and you need to reconsider your motivation.

Snap Out of It!

Remember: Do not read ahead. Set this book in full view so you will remember to keep your journal.

• • •

Your Journal

As you spend the next three days or more with the band, return to this space each night to note any reactions or feelings you have about the band, the program, or the goal you have chosen. Do you understand Snap and Stop? Are you committed to proceed? What percentage of the time are you succeeding with Snap and Stop?

• • •

_____

_____

_____

_____

_____

_____

_____

CHAPTER SEVEN
Mastering Relaxation

Read this chapter as part of Step 4.

Before you start learning this step, you should feel very, very comfortable with Snap and Stop, which you learned in the previous chapter. If you are not snapping and thinking "stop" as described, then you need to go back to chapter 6, reread it, and practice the technique.

So now you have learned to Snap and Stop and you are ready to move on to the next step of Snap Out of It—relax. And, again as you did in the previous chapters, I want you to read this chapter only, practicing what you have learned for three days to two weeks. Do not skip ahead.

Snap Out of It!

Remember: Note your progress and feelings in the journal space provided on page 88.

• • •

Researchers who have studied people in the process of transitioning from one behavior to another have found that they are often subject to an added problem. You may be experiencing it now. You're comfortable or familiar with being one way so there's a pull to stay at that place but, at the same time, there's the push not to. Psychologists recognize and describe this situation with the term "conflict."

"No kidding," you're probably thinking. "Tell me about it." Truth be told, conflict creates stress. So now you know why you're probably feeling stressed.

Studies have shown that in stressful situations when you make adjustments in your behavior, your blood pressure is elevated and other physiological changes take place. This has been referred to as the "fight-or-flight" response, first described by Dr. Walter B. Cannon of the Harvard Medical School. It is a primitive response that our ancestors needed for survival.

Today we're not in the same survival mode, although we

may feel like it. Your boss says something that disturbs you; you feel like you're about to explode, and you want to scream at him. Of course that would be "socially inappropriate"— and besides, you'd get in trouble. If we fight we're working against ourselves. If we withdraw, we usually haven't solved anything and it's very likely that we only intensify those stressful feelings. So what do we do with the stress?

You can prevent or control the stress by learning how to relax. You need not be a victim. As Dr. Benson has explained, not only is the relaxation response innate, but the physiologic changes it produces are opposite to those produced by the fight-or-flight mode. It's not an automatic reaction but it can be elicited in a simple manner; with practice, it can become effortless.

For many of us, being anxious and tense is part of the way we always operate. It's often so much a part of us that we sometimes forget that there's another way to feel. Anxiety and tension seem almost prevalent in our modern society. Therefore, relaxation usually has to be learned.

A few of my patients are so tense they don't know if they are relaxed or not. Here are a few questions that will help you think about whether or not you are relaxed.

Snap Out of It!

- Is my body tense?

- Have I smiled recently? Laughed?

- Am I sleeping well?

- Am I able to enjoy leisure activities?

- Do I fidget? Am I tapping my foot constantly?

Relaxation means "letting go." You will have to practice this step more than the proceeding steps. At first you might be skeptical, but trust me, you *can* learn to relax.

I felt the same skepticism when I tried to learn to play tennis. I thought, "How can I do this? Nothing comes naturally. I have to remember to do all these things at once!" I had to think about everything I was doing. But guess what? The more I practiced, the less I had to concentrate on what I was doing. Some of the moves started to come automatically.

And this is similar to how learning relaxation will work. At first learning to relax will seem awkward, unnatural, and ultimately unattainable. But if you persist with practice, you should begin to notice little changes.

Once you learn the relaxation step, you will have mastered four steps in the process:

Step 1: You have chosen your goal.

Step 2: You have become familiar with your band.

Step 3: You have learned Snap and Stop.

Step 4: You have learned ways to relax.

Not bad! Only two more steps to learn. You should start to notice some difference in the way you feel and act.

With the addition of this step, you will remind yourself to use a relaxation technique after the Snap and Stop. Some people, like my patient Becca, use a sigh or a deep breath as a signal to relax, or simply utter the word itself.

"When I start worrying about my job, I snap the band and I automatically think "Stop," but I also take a deep breath and let all the tension out as I let myself relax," explains

Snap Out of It!

Becca. "I can almost feel my body releasing the pent-up energy."

Becca's method for relaxing is used in many techniques. For instance, during labor, the mother is told to focus on her breathing. Perhaps one big sigh isn't enough, and you may need to focus on the breathing as a new mother does. Think "Relax" as you focus on your breathing.

One of my other patients uses this moment to smile. There have been numerous studies demonstrating that just the act of smiling makes you feel happier. I even have one patient who imagines herself skiing when she needs to relax. If you don't ski, you can imagine yourself doing your favorite activity, whether it is walking on the beach, playing basketball, or gardening. You are aiming for a sense of release, calm, clarity of thought, or flow.

Wes, another patient, likes to stretch or just shake out his muscles in order to relax. This also works very well. It is very difficult to be relaxed emotionally if your muscles are all tensed up. Wes rotates his head, stretches his arms above his head, stands up and shakes out his hands. If he is in a meeting, or some other public place, he will just arch his back, sit up straight, and move his shoulders up and down.

Step 4: Relax

Try it and see if you don't feel at least a little less stressed.

As you've been reading, you may have been thinking, "So how does this all work?" Even though we're going slowly, you might feel a little overwhelmed. At this point it's reassuring to see how easy it is for Karen. She combines all three of the above methods as part of her relaxing stage. Her example may help to clarify the process for you.

"When I start to think about having a cigarette, I snap my band and say, 'No'." Then I'll take a couple of deep breaths while I stretch, and I immediately feel less anxious, more relaxed." Karen said. "Actually, I hadn't really thought about it before, but when I'm relaxed, I think more clearly and with perspective. I don't compulsively reach for that cigarette. I guess I'm sort of saying 'Hey, wait a minute . . .' to myself."

"Bingo!" I told her. "Now you understand what the Snap Out of It technique can really do for you. It will give you time to relax and think about what you're doing, or are about to do."

Karen continued, "I used to feel the need to smoke a cigarette, particularly when I was anxious. So, without thinking, I would grab the cigarette just to get a sense of relief from the stress. Then, for about ten minutes, I would feel relaxed.

Snap Out of It!

And then. . . ."

"And then what would happen?" I asked.

"And then I would hate myself for breaking my promise to give up smoking."

"So you only felt better for ten minutes, and then the stress came back worse then ever." I said.

"That's right." She agreed. "I thought I was relieving the stress, but I only got a ten minute high that was replaced with a feeling of despair that lasted all day," Karen explained. "I felt like I was in a no-win situation, and that I was weak and powerless to change. I would try hard for a while and try to be 'perfect,' but it would never last very long."

"Learning to relax was important for me," she continued, "because it's always been so hard for me to stop smoking, due to my compulsive temperament. It was hard for me to learn to stop, relax, and think about my actions, and I found that the relaxing helped me to reconsider and reflect on what I was about to do."

• • •

The more Karen practiced the Snap Out of It technique, the more she found herself automatically trying to relax in any situation. According to Karen, she felt "more relaxed a great deal of the time." This, as mentioned previously, is an added benefit of practicing the Snap Out of It technique, and who doesn't want to feel more relaxed?

In fact, if you are relaxed, you'll find that many things in your life will become easier—things such as problem-solving, sports, relationships, and getting a good night's rest, among others.

Some of my patients practice this relaxation exercise as part of a bigger effort by spending five to ten minutes a day concentrating on relaxing and letting go. Jerry just shuts his office door and sits quietly, closes his eyes, and imagines himself lying in the sun on the deck of a boat, rocking gently with the waves. This gives him strength to face the rest of the day. Jerry says that he knows that whatever happens at work, there's a Jerry who can't be touched, happily lying in the sun.

In fact why don't you try it right now! Here's how:

1. First, find a comfortable, quiet spot. You should be sitting or lying down.

Snap Out of It!

2. Shrug your shoulders up and down several times. Shake out the stress in your back. Relax your hands on your lap, or place them across your abdomen if you are lying down.

3. Close your eyes and focus on your breathing. As you breath in, think about breathing calm thoughts into your body; when you exhale, imagine yourself letting go of the stress.

4. Let yourself flow with the breathing. Don't let any negative thoughts into your brain. Picture yourself in a field of wildflowers, on the beach, or just floating.

5. Keep this up for five to ten minutes, or until you feel the tension flow from your body.

• • •

There are important scientific reasons why taking a deep breath helps you to relax. Even small changes in your brain's oxygen level can affect the way you feel and act. You should be breathing mostly from your abdomen, but many of us incorrectly breathe by raising their chest. This is shallow breathing, which will ultimately deprive your brain of much needed oxygen, causing you to become irritable and tense.

To practice breathing more efficiently, place your hand on your belly and try to move it up and down as you slowly breathe. If you can't feel the difference, try lying down on your bed with a coin placed on your bellybutton. As you breathe, concentrate on making the coin move up and down. Breathing correctly is a large part of relaxation through Yoga.

You can practice breathing correctly whenever you have some free time. Some of my patients use a computer for a good part of their day, and they find that they can actually practice their stretching and breathing as they work. When my patient Rick gets bored during a long meeting at the office, he concentrates on his breathing. Rick tells me that this has an added benefit, in that he doesn't feel as exhausted and frustrated by the two hour meeting he's had to endure. For some of you, the whole experience of trying to relax may be difficult. Pat was having this problem.

• • •

Snap Out of It!

"Dr. Cohen, I've tried all the breathing exercises. I've tried to imagine myself floating. Nothing works, when I snap the band I can say, "Stop," but I can't relax," she complained.

"What seems to get in your way?" I asked.

"It's my boyfriend, I can't stop thinking about how inconsiderate he is to me."

"Pat, you need to let go of the tension." I said.

"I just can't. I'm too angry." She replied.

• • •

In this case, Pat's anger is preventing her from being able to use the relaxation technique. What she needs to do is to let go of her anger. She can do this by acknowledging what it is that is making her angry, admitting to herself that her anger has a big negative influence on her happiness, and consciously deciding to let go. Once she makes the decision that she needs to just let go of her negative feelings, she will be able to relax. She needs to be persistent.

"Pat, you need to re-snap, say 'Stop' again, and try to relax a second or third time, each time reminding yourself to let go of your anger." I said. "Try emptying your mind of any type of negative thought at all. Take a deep breath each time, and by the third deep breath and sigh, you should find yourself close to relaxed—if only for a short time. Promise me you'll try this for two weeks."

Pat promised, and after two weeks she was much better at relaxing after she said the word "Stop." (She admitted at first she had to say ". . . stop. Stop! *Stop!*") In fact, it seemed to me that her face appeared to be less tense in general.

●　●　●

I've used the term "letting go" in several places. That's what many of us have to do in order to relax. Some of us find it difficult to let go. Either it's hard to rid ourselves of an emotion like anger, or we're afraid to be in a situation where we're not constantly on guard. We somehow feel that relaxing makes us vulnerable, that we lose control.

I saw this repeatedly when conducting stress management workshops for various corporations. I often used an exercise that required participants to use visualization as a method of relaxation. They were asked to close their eyes while they imagined certain pleasant scenes. Inevitably, there was always a small contingent of people who would not participate. When I asked why, they couldn't immediately tell me, but after many such discussions with dozens of groups, the bottom line was always a kind of anxiety, fear, or guilt.

Anxiety, fear, and guilt are emotions that block some people from relaxing. If you're afraid of losing control, or if you are feeling guilty, you may not even be in touch with these emotions. The questions that follow will help you to put these feelings into perspective with the aim of letting them go.

1. What do I think will happen to me if I let myself relax?

2. Can I see or feel that a relaxation mode is a safe place to be?

3. Does feeling relaxed make me feel guilty?

4. Can I see or feel that feeling relaxed is productive?

5. Do I think that I have other things to do that are more important than feeling relaxed?

6. Can I see why it is important that feeling relaxed be made a priority?

7. Does feeling relaxed take away my anger?

8. Can I see or feel that when I'm relaxed I am better able to deal with my anger?

9. Am I afraid that people will take advantage of me if I am not all churned up and tense?

10. Can I see or feel that being relaxed widens rather than restricts my options?

11. Do I feel worthy only when I am pleasing someone else?

12. Can I see that feeling relaxed is important for me and that I deserve it?

If you're still having a problem, answer the one big question, "What's so good about being relaxed?" When you are

Snap Out of It!

relaxed, you are in charge. By relaxing you have taken control—taken a positive action towards change. It may sound contradictory, but being relaxed is a powerful position to be in. It means you are master of your own emotions, that no one or thing is controlling your feelings. When you are relaxed you are not in the grips of emotions such as anger, fear, anxiety, and guilt.

When you are relaxed you are open to change and your long-term goal. By taking control of your emotions you have made something happen, and that means you have power—power to change and power to achieve your goal.

In fact, once you feel you have managed to let go, here are some ways to maximize or extend your blissful period of relaxation:

- Smile; stretch.

- Call a friend.

- Take a walk, even if it's just down the office hall.

- Accomplish something, even if it's only an errand.

Step 4: Relax

• Read a good book, or a fun magazine.

• Hug someone.

• • •

Hey—strangely enough, you'll find you might really get to like being relaxed!

• • •

Try the following exercises and see if you positively affect your mood and/or any part of your body:

• Stretch out your back. Arch your back, and then raise your shoulders up to your ears.

• Rotate your neck in a circle.

• Stretch your fingers wide, reach as far above your head as you can. Interlock the fingers of one hand with your other hand and push away from your chest. If you are sitting in a chair, stretch your legs out in front of you and move your feet back and forth in the air, pointing your toes.

Snap Out of It!

With the Snap Out of It technique, you are learning to relax on cue. Your cue is the Stop and Snap steps. Without this cue, I find that most patients practice relaxing for a day or two and then slide right back into their old pattern of stress and anxiety. They simply forget about relaxing. How can they remember to relax when they are fretting about an injustice or a fear? With the stress comes the self- medication behaviors such as smoking and eating.

Here the band is also useful as a reminder to stretch and breath deeply. I find that if you happen to be doing something and you see the band on your wrist, you will be reminded to take a deep breath and stretch; in doing so, you will experience a slight lift in your mood. Or perhaps your back will thank you. This is called positive reinforcement. If something gives you pleasure you will do it again and again- which means the next time you look at your band, you'll remember to relax even if you weren't implementing the six-step technique. This has very big advantages.

Now, once again, you will have to put the book down and practice your new step for at least three days and up to two weeks.

Step 4: Relax

• • •

Remember:

1. Put this book where you will see it, and use the journal on the following page daily.

2. Do not proceed to the next chapter before you have mastered relaxation.

• • •

As you practice make sure you are incorporating all the steps you have worked on to date:

Step 1: You have chosen your goal.

Step 2: You have become familiar with your band.

Step 3: You have learned Snap and Stop.

Step 4: Practice relaxing and letting go.

You can do it!

Snap Out of It!

Your Journal

Are you taking deep breaths after you say "Stop"? Sit up straight and smile. Let go! Do you feel less tense? Write how you felt as you relaxed. Did you feel differently?

•   •   •

_____

_____

_____

_____

_____

_____

_____

_____

_____

_____

_____

Step 4: Relax

_____

_____

_____

_____

_____

_____

_____

_____

_____

_____

_____

_____

_____

_____

_____

_____

CHAPTER EIGHT
Start Talking to Yourself

Read this chapter as part of Step 5.

If you are beginning this chapter, then you have learned the relaxation step described in the previous chapter. I don't expect that you have learned how to relax all the time, but I do expect you know how to relax for a few minutes in conjunction with snapping and saying "stop." And, in just being able to learn to relax for a few minutes, you have accomplished something powerful. Just look around you at how many people aren't relaxed—it's not easy, but it sure feels good. And the more you practice, the better you'll feel.

If you don't have this feeling, I recommend you do not proceed and keep practicing the previous steps to the technique.

Snap Out of It!

Work on your deep breathing, stretching, and letting go.

Do you feel ready to start talking to yourself? I hope so, because that's the next step in the Snap Out of It technique. It's a technique commonly referred to as self talk, and it is the basis of many self-help books. Call it self-talk, inner tapes, your script, etc.—it's all the same. We are constantly talking to ourselves or, in other words, thinking to ourselves. We are processing our thoughts in a type of self-talk.

Self-talk is a part of the field of cognitive psychology. Cognitive psychology has taken a central place in the type of mental health treatment that is currently provided. Its premise is that the way we think determines how we feel. Let me give you an example.

Susan lost her job. She told me that she would never find another one like it. Maybe she wouldn't even find a new job at all. She ruminated about how unfair life was. She felt distraught.

Myrna also lost her job to downsizing. She wasn't happy about it, but then she said, "Wow. This is really an opportunity for me to pursue something on my own." She felt elated.

Both Myrna and Susan worked for the same company and had the same thing happen to them. But look at the difference in their reactions. If you reread the above examples it becomes obvious—what they say to themselves determines how they feel and what they do. Susan is dejected and stuck. Myrna is happy and ready to move forward.

Why do these two people respond in such an opposite manner? According to cognitive psychologists we have different belief systems with different messages. Most likely these were learned from our parents or other significant people in our lives. Do you see the glass as half-empty or half-full? How we process that information depends upon our beliefs about life and people.

Susan believed that the world was unfair and that she was a victim. Myrna believed that things don't always turn out the way that you expect, but that you can use them to your advantage.

On many occasions, I have had people in my office who complained about bad marriages, horrendous work situations, or friends and relatives who were taking advantage of them. Yet, they were frozen. They could address the issues that were making them miserable, but they were unable to do anything about them.

They told themselves they weren't worthy enough to ask

for something different. Or they were afraid that they would be rejected. Or it was too hard to change. Or. . . .

In order to change, you need to examine what you say to yourself. You need to re-record those old stale tapes in your head. Get rid of your negative self-defeating thoughts and change or replace these old tapes with positive ones. This is called cognitive restructuring.

In traditional therapy, we analyze those messages and find their source. We understand how and why they have a grip on us and discover how they relate to our backgrounds. It's helpful to know where your messages come from, but in behavior therapy you don't need to know how and why these beliefs were formed. You simply need to discover what they are, accept them, change them, and move on.

• • •

Albert Ellis, a pioneer in the field of cognitive psychology, described ten basic fundamental beliefs people have that work against them. Among them are the following ideas:

- I expect other people to behave the way I think they should; it's terrible when they do not.

Step 5: Talk to Yourself

- I have certain expectations for how I should behave, and I should always act that way.

- I just react to things that happen around me; the events cause me to be miserable.

If you have these beliefs, you will be constantly disappointed. They are unrealistic. Dr. Ellis explains why they are impossible to achieve or how they will cause you to behave in ways that are detrimental.

Perhaps you can see why these thoughts would be nonproductive. On the other hand, perhaps some of these statements are like your own. "What's wrong," you ask, "with having expectations for always behaving a certain way?"

If you have an expectation that you should always act a certain way, you probably don't forgive yourself when you make a mistake. Contrast this idea with the following thoughts:

- I'm not perfect. I'm allowed to make mistakes.

- I can learn from my mistakes.

Snap Out of It!

- I understand situations are different. It is easier to act a certain way in some circumstances than in others.

These thoughts are more freeing, less judgmental. They invite new ways of feeling. They open up, rather than restrict, new avenues of behaving.

When I encourage some of my patients to take a positive stance, they sometimes resist. Often the comment is, "I can't do anything about my problem," or "I don't have any luck." With that type of self-talk, you are absolutely blocked from taking any positive action.

That type of thinking is bound to lead to failure. Over the course of years, working with people, I have found that there's a list of "warning words." When I hear these words, I know that we need to change the messages. Negative thoughts can be automatic and almost an easy way out. Negative thoughts give you an excuse for not succeeding or making an effort to do something.

Watch out for these words:

- Can't

- Not able to

Step 5: Talk to Yourself

- It's futile

- It's too hard

- I don't have the patience

- I know I'll fail

- It's not important

- But

These negative messages can be changed into positive ones.

Negative: I can't exercise. I have no inner discipline.
Positive: I haven't exercised, but I'm going to take myself seriously enough to start now.

Negative: I'm not able to stop worrying.
Positive: I haven't stopped worrying yet because I haven't had the right tools. Now I know I can be successful.

Negative: It's futile. Every time I take off weight, I put it back on.

Snap Out of It!

Positive: If I approach dieting in a systematic way, I can keep the weight off.

Negative: It's too hard to meet people.
Positive: There are organizations I can join to meet people. I just need to find out what they are.

Negative: I know I'll fail because I can never stick with it.
Positive: I've failed in the past, but I can learn from my failures and try again.

Negative: I don't have the patience to keep trying.
Positive: I know that by persisting I will be successful.

Negative: It's not important to get ahead.
Positive: I feel good enough about myself to succeed and I deserve it.

Negative: I want to control my anger, but now is not the right time to start working on it.
Positive: I want to control my anger, and I'll start a week from Tuesday.

Step 5: Talk to Yourself

It has been found (no surprise) that people who learn to challenge negative self-talk and instead learn to rethink in a positive manner are much more successful in what they do. Their body chemistry is altered, blood pressure is reduced, cholesterol is lowered, and endorphins are increased so that they feel better both physically and psychologically.

We need lots of practice unlearning old thoughts and replacing them with new ways of thinking about things. The more accustomed you become to breaking the old pattern, the easier it will be to have new, uplifting messages.

But before we can change our messages, we have to know what they are. Most often we're not aware of our negative thinking or we don't understand how it contributes to our behavior.

• • •

Helen feels badly when she doesn't contribute at meetings. As a child, her mother always made negative comments about what she had to say and criticized her friends. Her self-esteem is terrible. She needs to erase her mother's voice in her head and substitute positive thoughts before she can

Snap Out of It!

ever hope to feel happy and positive enough about herself to succeed.

"I want to get ahead at work and speak up at meetings, but I freeze," she complained.

"What are you thinking when you freeze?" I asked.

"I'm thinking that what I have to say is not important. That I'm foolish to think someone like me can get ahead," Helen explained.

"You see, Helen, you've been playing your mother's *tape*. And you've been living that *tape*. You need to listen to another *tape*."

Jack had a similar problem that was also holding him back in everything he did. He could never bring himself to ask out women he liked on a date. He'd been an unpopular kid in high school, but all of a sudden, at twenty-nine, he became a very successful businessman who looked quite confident in a pinstriped suit. But Jack still carried around the image of the unpopular kid in his head. He expected that no woman would be interested in him, despite the fact that many often flirted with him. Jack needed a new image, and I told him he could change his negative feelings about himself by picturing a new Jack.

Step 5: Talk to Yourself

"Jack, you need to talk to yourself," I coached.

"What?" he asked.

"Talk to yourself," I repeated. "It's generally called self-talk. You need to tell yourself how great you are. You're not that little boy in fifth grade any more. You're a successful businessman. Think about what you have to offer."

"I know I have a good income . . ." he said, then he paused.

"You have more than that," I pushed. "What else?"

"Um, I like animals, children. And I like to go dancing and to the movies . . . and people tell me I'm very generous. They also tell me I have a good sense of humor."

"Do you believe them when they say those things about you?" I asked.

"No, but I'd like to," he said quietly.

I suggested that he spend the next two to three days, being aware of any negative thoughts that he had. I asked him to write these down on a piece of paper and when and where they happened. Jack was shocked to discover how many negative thoughts he had about his abilities, his image, and his personality.

"No wonder I'm reluctant to approach women. I'm more

negative about myself than I realized," he reported. "I never knew how self-deprecating my thoughts had been—and not just in regard to dating. For instance, Dr. Cohen, when I looked in my closet this morning, I saw a mess and I immediately thought, 'Boy am I a slob.' And then when I realized I was five minutes late in leaving the house to catch the train, I thought, 'I can't plan my time.' I was amazed to discover that I had these thoughts throughout the day. I was being unnaturally hard on myself. No wonder I get depressed. I'm giving myself criticism all day long. Who needs that?"

"As you discovered Jack, many of us are our own worst critic."

Are you your own worst critic?

If you constantly criticized a child without giving any positive feedback, you would expect that child to develop a poor self-image. You would also expect that child to lack motivation. He would be afraid to experiment, feeling sure that he would fail.

It's strange—we all seem to understand that it helps to praise a child, encourage a child rather than to constantly criticize a child. But when it comes to ourselves, we forget

Step 5: Talk to Yourself

our own egos can be dramatically affected by what we say to ourselves.

If you are constantly criticizing yourself, most likely you had parents or other significant people in your life who were overly critical of you or of themselves. You developed this same way of thinking without being aware of the damage it was causing.

As a young adult, I had many doubts about myself. I was driven to succeed, which I attributed to a normal, healthy desire to be successful. I worked and worked, but I wasn't happy; what I accomplished was never enough to make me feel good about myself.

People would tell me how successful I was, but I didn't really feel it inside. I was clueless to the idea that I was too critical of myself.

Gradually I began to realize that my constant need to succeed as an adult was really a response to the messages I received from my overly critical mother when I was growing up. These were messages such as:

• "Enough is never enough."

Snap Out of It!

- "You can always try a little bit harder."

- "You must do your very best."

- "If you fail, it's because you did something wrong."

These were her own messages to herself as well. My mother was hard on herself and was never satisfied. As a child, I could never please my mother, consequently, I also learned to never be pleased with myself. Interesting how I repeated my mother's pattern.

My mother had never accepted failure. I was taught that it was my fault when I became ill. As an adult I naturally felt that if I got sick, then I must be weak.

A more self-accepting person might think, "I caught this cold from the waitress who coughed all over me." I thought, "I caught this cold because I didn't take better care of myself. It's my own fault."

Today I know better and, when I catch a cold, I think to myself, "Well, lots of people have colds this month. I could have gotten it at the movies."

My thought pattern was similar to Jack's described earlier. Remember when Jack opened his closet in the morning? He saw the mess and thought to himself "I'm a slob." Jack needs to give himself a break. A more positive attitude would be to think:

"Hey, this closet is a mess, but I'm so busy with my work schedule it will have to wait until I have some free time."

or if neat closets aren't really important to Jack, then he could say:

"Closets aren't my strong point, and I consider it an accomplishment that at least my clothes aren't in piles on the floor."

You may be having a problem with this concept. Many mothers justify criticizing their children by saying, "It's only for your own good." Consequently, many people grow up believing that self-criticism is a good practice. Sometimes it can be, but a good deal of the time it can be very destructive in terms of a person's confidence and happiness.

Nadine was chronically unhappy with her husband, her

children, and her job. She was also unhappy with herself. She had a list of things for her family and herself to improve upon.

In each session with her, I would hear her list of improvements to be made: "My children need to read more books. My husband needs to be more vocal at work. I need to exercise more. . . ," and on and on it went.

"Nadine," I asked, "why aren't you ever happy with your children and husband and yourself? Does everything always have to be improved upon?"

She stared back at me blankly.

I prodded, "Why so many criticisms of your family? Can't you say anything good about them or yourself?"

She looked at me in disbelief: "What are you talking about?" she said.

"Can't you see that you're always criticizing your family and yourself? Are you unhappy with them?"

Nadine looked puzzled. "I'm criticizing them because I love them. It's for their own good. If my mother hadn't done the same for me, I probably wouldn't have finished high school."

• • •

Step 5: Talk to Yourself

This is the type of backwards thinking that makes negative thoughts seem like positive thoughts. And yet this is an extremely common way to view negative thinking. You may be one of the people who have a hard time even recognizing negative thoughts because you've been brainwashed into thinking that criticism is righteous and that it's the only way to improve yourself and others.

Words like "should", "must", and "have to" are often found in this type of negative self-criticism. Sometimes such words as "never" and "always" show up. Here are some examples of negative thoughts masquerading as positive criticism:

"Getting a B on a test is not good enough."

"I should dress more professionally for the office."

"I have to keep the house spotless."

While all of the above may be good ideas, there is no need to make them "rules." This makes our responses to them inflexible and leads to feelings of guilt or anger. I saw a family where the children complained that their mother was always cleaning the kitchen floor. They were afraid to make anything dirty, and that made them very tense.

Here is a better way to think about self-improvements.

"If I get a B on a test it isn't the end of the world."

"It will improve my image if I dress more professionally for the office."

"This week I may have time to vacuum the house only once."

Can you see the difference? The difference has to do with the "spin" that is put on the situation. Often you can turn your negative thoughts into positive thoughts by the simple turn of a phrase, which will challenge your initial emphasis. Something that once seemed so overpowering can take on a new less crucial light when it is rephrased.

· · ·

Are you beginning to get the feel for how you can change self-defeating thoughts into positive ones?

Step 5: Talk to Yourself

It's been my experience that lots of examples help to give you a handle on rewriting those old messages. The following illustrations are taken from people I have worked with who were successful in making the change.

Negative: I'm a lousy son. I can never remember my mom's birthday. And she gets so hurt when I don't send her a card.
Positive: I need to write down these special dates. I can even keep some cards on hand to use so I don't have to go out and buy them.

Negative: I hate working at Anderson but I won't leave because I might not like a new job any better.
Positive: I'll never know if I could be happier at a new job unless I try it.

Negative: I'm short; no one wants to date me.
Positive: I have a lot to share with someone who likes to read and cook.

Negative: It's necessary for me to call my mother-in-law, but I can't do it because she doesn't like me.

Positive: I'll call my mother-in-law whether she likes me or not. I'm a good person; if she doesn't like me, that's her problem.

Negative: My supervisor makes more money and gets all the credit for the things I do. I'm afraid to complain to the boss because he might not believe me.

Positive: I'll document all my work to show to the boss, and then I'll ask for a promotion because I deserve it.

Negative: I didn't get all I wanted to get done today.

Positive: I didn't get everything done, but I did the best I could. I'll prioritize things for tomorrow.

POSITIVE THINKING

A basketball or football coach tells his team that they will succeed. He is using positive thinking.

When a minister tells the congregation that they can

lead fuller and better lives, she is using positive thinking to motivate people to believe in themselves. Her messages are full of hope and salvation.

The best school teachers encourage their students to experiment and stretch. They reassure them that setbacks are an acceptable part of the process.

Think about the words you most like to hear from your spouse, your friends, or your boss. They are words of praise: they are positive words.

Surely you find yourself smiling when someone says to you, "You did a good job."

When someone compliments me, it gives me a little boost. If someone says, "Hey, you look great in that sweater," I stand up a little straighter.

But why wait for the busy people around you to stop what they are doing to compliment you? Wouldn't it be better if you could compliment yourself? If you learn to automatically replace negative thoughts with positive thoughts you will be, in effect, complimenting yourself. As a result, you'll be basking in a warm glow. You'll be your own coach and cheerleading squad; consequently, you'll be smiling a lot more and standing straighter.

This takes practice, but I can guarantee you that it is possible. In fact, some research shows that by thinking negative thoughts you will actually change your brain chemistry and become more depressed due to an imbalance of the chemicals that affect your mood. Conversely, researchers also believe that you can positively affect your moods by smiling and laughing. Studies have shown that the more you smile, the happier you will feel.

If you are skeptical that negative thoughts affect you, just think about how your body felt the last time you were tense or angry. One of my patients, Alice, had frequent headaches and neck aches. She had gone to many experts—from allergists to chiropractors—without relief. It wasn't until I taught her to use the Snap Out of It method that she began to physically feel better. Alice was learning to replace her negative angry thoughts with optimistic thoughts. And, as she did, her physical symptoms became less and less frequent.

"I was actually poisoning myself," Alice told me in amazement.

"Yes, you'd be surprised at how people can make themselves sick with negative thoughts. I have patients who have constant fatigue, debilitating diarrhea, and chronic sleep-lessness because they have upset their brain and body chemistry with their negative thinking."

In fact, the National Institute of Mental Health has stud-ied the effect of a person's mental thoughts upon the limbic system. The limbic system is the part of your brain that sets your emotional tone by storing extreme emotional memories, filtering external events, controlling appetite and sleep, and regulating libido. Researcher Dr. Mark George found that when his subjects entertained happy thoughts there was a cooling in their deep limbic system, whereas negative thoughts increased the activity of the limbic system.

• • •

Hopefully, you're now convinced of the importance of pos-itive self-talk, but you're not sure where to start. Relax, have fun; it's enjoyable to write down your positive tapes. It's good practice that will get you accustomed to thinking in a positive manner.

Mark once complained to me that his life was like that cartoon where he was always walking under a cloud. No matter where he went, the cloud followed him and rained on his parade. I told Mark that he needed an umbrella—something to protect him from the rain, something he could use until the cloud disappeared.

His umbrella was constructed with his positive thoughts. These positive thoughts are often referred to as affirmations. You don't always have to wait, nor should you wait, until you have a negative thought in order to tell yourself something positive and uplifting. Here are examples of some affirmations you can tell yourself anytime:

- I am lovable.

- I am a giving person. I like to help others.

- I work hard at work and at home.

- I'm a good parent.

- I'm an excellent baker. No one can beat my chocolate cake.

Step 5: Talk to Yourself

I want you to take the next few days to think about all the good things that pertain to your life. And when you get up in the morning and look in the mirror, remember to compliment yourself. Tell yourself something nice about how you look, or what you do, or the kind of person that you are. This will get you ready for positive self-talk.

• • •

Remember: Keep practicing your other steps. Don't forget to say "Stop", snap the band, and relax.

• • •

Your Journal

Use the following pages to write down your affirmations.

_____

_____

_____

_____

Snap Out of It!

Mr. Donald Nemczuk
15 Lawler Ln.
Norwich, CT 06360

_____

_____

_____

_____

_____

_____

_____

_____

_____

_____

_____

_____

_____

_____

_____

_____

_____

Step 5: Talk to Yourself

Now you're ready!

It is very important to understand that to succeed at Step 5, you must feel comfortable with the following four very important steps:

Step 1: You have chosen a goal.

Step 2: You have become familiar with your band.

Step 3: You have learned Snap and Stop.

Step 4: You know how to relax.

Now let's proceed to learn how to change the way to talk to yourself.

Step 5. You will learn positive self-talk.

Don't assume you can accomplish Step 5 in a matter of days. It will take at least two weeks of constantly monitoring your own thoughts to even make an inroad into mastering the

Snap Out of It!

art of changing your thoughts. Remember, I said that the first step in changing your negative thoughts is to discover what negative tapes you are playing. Think of yourself as a heat-seeking missile. The negative thoughts are your enemy, not your friend. You're going to zero in on them so you can erase them and record over them.

Your Journal

I want you to think about your goal. Now use the following three pages to write down any negative thoughts that you have had over the past 2–3 days. I also want you to write down the circumstances you were in when you had the thought. Focus on how you felt. Now you're ready for Step 5.

• • •

_____

_____

_____

_____

Step 5: Talk to Yourself

Snap Out of It!

RE-RECORDING YOUR TAPE.

You need a procedure for looking at your journal entries. There are four key elements.

1. Look carefully at what you have written.

2. Define when and why you had a problem.

3. Describe your self-talk. Were you judgmental? What did you worry about? What did you assume might happen?

4. Describe your feelings.

Now you can commit to making a change. Ask yourself: What could I say to myself that would make me feel better? How can I be less judgmental of myself? How can I make my negative predictions or assumptions into positive ones? As Dr. Ellis, the noted therapist, advises, you need to dispute and challenge those ideas that are causing you defeat.

I want you to be sure you're focusing on your thoughts in

Step 5: Talk to Yourself

an analytical way. When something comes into your mind in response to a situation or person, take the time to analyze whether or not the thoughts you are having are negative in their approach. Then try to figure out how you can neutralize them or change them into positive thoughts.

Here's a chance to use that umbrella. If you're having difficulty thinking of something positive, think of your affirmations. You deserve to succeed—you're a very unique and special person.

You may also find it helpful to challenge your negative thoughts with questions and think of alternative actions. All it takes is a little creativity and lots of practice. For instance:

Negative: "That woman is attractive, but she'd never talk to me if I approach her."

Challenge: "If she's not friendly, that's her problem; I'll just excuse myself."

Negative: "I'd better not confront my boss. He may be angry."

Challenge: "Don't I have a right to express my opinion? Maybe I can do it in a way that's not threatening."

Snap Out of It!

In the process of thinking about your alternatives, you may find a way to improve upon a situation. This in itself will help you to relieve some of the stress and help to prevent you from losing sight of your goal.

Remember, you have choice. You don't need to repeat old patterns and keep getting stuck. So get out your creative thinking cap and trade in your old tapes for some bright shiny new CDs.

By the way, it also helps to try to avoid negative people. Do you have a friend who's always complaining? If so, you should cut down on the amount of time you spend with that person. If, on the other hand, there is someone who makes you laugh, I would go out of my way to make time for that person. Feeling down? Take the time to walk down the hall to see a colleague who always has a smile for you.

I want you to practice self-talk for one to two weeks. You should also be practicing the other steps of the Snap Out of It technique.

1. Remember your primary goal. Keep it in the forefront.

2. Wear your band constantly.

Step 5: Talk to Yourself

3. Continue to snap and say/think "Stop."

4. Relax with deep breathing and stretching.

5. Practice positive self-talk.

It is important you continue to keep your journal during these weeks as you learn self-talk. So keep this book in a place where you will see it—on your kitchen table, by your bed, or on your desk.

Think of the steps in the Snap Out of It technique as the foundation. Each step is a building block upon which the other steps depend. If you have a weak step, the whole structure will be unsteady and may ultimately fall.

CHAPTER NINE
Putting It All Together

Read this Chapter as Part of Step 6.

Congratulations! You have made it to the last step: Step 6, Putting It All Together.

So you've set your goal, you've practiced snapping your band, you've learned to relax, and you're aware of your negative self-talk. Those are big accomplishments. Essentially, you have new skills to put into action that are alternatives to old ways of thinking and behaving.

You may have found that practicing each skill has had a positive effect on you. Now let's put them all together.

Suppose you want to lose weight: when you start focusing on the piece of chocolate or eating between meals, snap your band and say, "Stop" either silently or out loud. Next relax, because already your body is stressed and you need to distance yourself in order to clarify your thinking. Then, through self-talk, restructure the way you've been looking at the situation.

• • •

Jessica is a good example of someone who learned to use the Snap Out of It technique successfully. When she came to see me, she was thirty pounds overweight and could never stay on a diet. At the time she was also suffering from headaches and neck pain that she never mentioned because she attributed them to physical causes. Jessica was having a problem dieting because she was using food to neutralize negative thoughts she unconsciously aimed at herself. Here is how the cycle is triggered:

Stressful Situation: Jessica's boss disagrees with her at a large company meeting.

Negative Thought Process: She immediately begins to think negative thoughts such as, "My boss must not like me," and "It was a stupid idea, I shouldn't have mentioned it in the meeting."

Step 6: Put It Together

Chemical Reaction: Her negative thoughts begin to cause a chemical reaction that leads to more negative thoughts and triggers a headache.

Self Medication (In this case, food)*:* Her limbic system has taken a nose dive, and she is desperate to relieve her suffering. So she does what she has always done in the past when she has felt so stressed—Jessica goes to the vending machine and eats a bag of potato chips. This gives her a temporary emotional lift, but she still has the headache.

Negative Thoughts Return: Jessica's lift is fleeting. Twenty minutes later, her negative thoughts return with a vengeance. And now there are more of them. Added to the stressful thoughts about her boss and the meeting are the feelings of guilt. She starts to think, "I shouldn't have eaten those chips. I can never stay on a diet. I'm fat; I'll always be fat."

More Negative Thoughts: Jessica's limbic system goes into another nose dive and her negative thoughts continue throughout the day. Her whole outlook is colored. She views everything else that occurs that day in a negative light. When her husband is late for dinner, she assumes it's because he doesn't really care about her feelings—when, in truth, he was caught in traffic.

Self Medication Continues: Jessica raids the cupboard for cookies as a relief from her bad feelings.

• • •

Now let's see how Jessica used the Snap Out of It technique to break her eating response.

Stressful Situation: Jessica's boss disagrees with her at a company meeting.

Negative Thought Process: She begins to have negative thoughts.

Thought-Stopping: She finds herself thinking about eating potato chips, and she uses the Snap Out of It technique by thinking, "Stop!" She forces the thoughts of both the bad meeting and eating aside.

Step 6: Put It Together

Snap the Band: She next snaps the band to remind herself of her dieting goal.

Relaxation: After snapping her band, she takes a deep breath and lets go of the frustration from the stressful meeting.

Self-Talk: She replaces her negative thoughts about the confrontation at the meeting with positive thoughts: "I know my idea is a good one. It's his problem if he can't understand it. I'll write a memo describing it in more detail."

• • •

Jessica made it through this stressful situation and stuck to her diet. Instead of trying to assuage her stressful feelings with food, she was able to gain control over her negative thoughts by employing the Snap Out of It plan. In the past she had turned to food as a crutch; now she had a plan she knew she could depend on to get her though her stressful situation.

As a result, she was inspired and happy for several reasons:

Snap Out of It!

- She was able to resist the urge to eat. Her diet was on track.

- She was able to overcome the negative obsessive thoughts and relax.

- She praised herself and came up with positive steps to take.

Jessica felt good about herself as a result of her success; the more she succeeded, the better she became at using the Snap Out of It technique. As the saying goes: "Nothing succeeds like success."

• • •

Reading Jessica's example may have left you feeling uneasy. I can hear you saying. "Oh, it's so complex or complicated." You may think, "How will I ever remember all the steps?"

Be reassured that combining all the steps simultaneously will become almost second nature. I've used the sports analogy in this book before, and it's a good one. Think back to other things you have learned in your past, like riding a

Step 6: Put It Together

bike, playing golf, using a computer or playing the guitar. At first, learning these skills probably felt overwhelming. Everything you did made you feel clumsy. You probably left things out and fell flat on your face. I know I have.

Cathy had been complaining in her weekly sessions that the Snap Out of It technique was difficult for her to master. "If I snap, I forget to think, 'Stop.' Or if I think, 'Stop,' I forget the self-talk."

"Cathy, have you ever learned a complex sport?" I asked.

"Well, let's see. I learned to cross-country ski approximately ten years ago," she replied.

"Try to remember your learning curve. How soon did you feel competent?"

"When I was first learning to cross-country ski, I was falling all over myself," she replied. "It was extremely frustrating. I was trying to move my legs and arms in an unfamiliar rhythm. And often I was trying to do this on very icy trails. I remember several hills where I became so exhausted from falling that I broke down and cried right there, lying in the snow. I must have been a sight."

"Well, it's good to see that you feel better about it now, Cathy."

Snap Out of It!

"In retrospect I can see that I did get progressively better. Now everything flows naturally. My movements have become second nature."

"You don't have to think about every step. You did once, and, in a sense you still are, but the steps have become internalized. Just like driving a car, you drive on a type of automatic pilot reflex. You don't think, "Now push on the brake pedal." You just automatically hit the brake when you have the right cues," I explained.

In the same manner that Cathy learned to ski, you'll find the technique will become easier. In fact, you'll want to make the Snap Out of It technique as automatic as driving a car. When you see a red light, you automatically step on the car's brake. You don't spend a lot of time thinking about the light or what your reaction should be. Trust me. You will become as comfortable with the technique if you make the effort to practice it as often as possible for several weeks.

"I almost quit," noted Cathy in wonder. "You know, I almost gave up on cross-country skiing. I'm so glad I didn't. I love to ski now."

"What kept you going? Why didn't you quit?" I asked.

She stopped and laughed. "I knew other people who had

learned to cross-country ski. And I could see improvement, slight improvement—but there was improvement."

"So you were encouraged by the slight improvement to keep trying."

"Yes, that was it. As long as I got even a tiny bit better each time I skied, I was encouraged to keep trying. There were even times that I wasn't as good, but I didn't let small set-backs discourage me."

• • •

One of the key points in Cathy's experience of learning a new sport was progress, even small progress. When she broke down crying, she didn't give up. She pulled herself up, literally, and tried again. She didn't give up in disgust. She saw improvement. She kept an open mind.

• • •

One of the reasons I wanted to keep this book short and to the point was because I wanted the Snap Out of It technique to be simple to learn. I believe the length of the book, it's directness, and the simplicity of the technique will encourage you to honestly try the plan as described.

Snap Out of It!

If you find a weak point you need to spend time rebuilding:

1. Go back to the appropriate chapter and reread the explanation.

2. Over emphasize this part of the technique while employing all the steps.

3. Devise little cues or tricks that may help you to implement this step.

4. Remind yourself that you need to master this step if you want to succeed in your goal to change your life.

The book is written in a way that makes it extremely easy for you flip back to any place and reread a section. There's nothing wrong with starting over at chapter 2, 3, or 4. It won't take much time to try again. You shouldn't feel intimidated to start again.

In fact, it would be a shame if you didn't. We've all heard the expression about getting right back in the saddle if you fall off a horse. And this is a very small pony to get back up on. Remember, Cathy kept getting back on her skis, and each time she did it was slightly easier than the last time. Each little improvement gave her hope. She was keeping a positive attitude. Though she didn't know it at the time, she was using positive self-talk to keep herself skiing. Instead of thinking "I'm a klutz, I'll never learn to ski," she thought "Hey, I went down that hill and I only fell once; not bad." Cathy was using Step 5, self-talk, to encourage herself.

• • •

Be careful. You may be tempted to skip one of the steps in the method. It may not be obvious at first why you need to have mastered each and every one of the steps to succeed. It wasn't obvious to Carlos. He decided that the snap step was the best step, and there was no reason to use the relaxation step.

"Carlos, you're a carpenter. Tell me something—when you're building a house, do you start with the second floor?" I asked.

"How could you do that?" he answered. "You know you have to build the first floor before you start the second. There's an order to building a house."

Snap Out of It!

"Well, what if I wanted to skip a part? What difference would it make?"

"Well, you could run into a lot of problems. Something would collapse, and you'd have to start all over from the beginning."

"Oh, I see. So, I'll have to start from Step One," I mused.

Carlos stared back at me and broke into a smile. "I see your point, Dr. Cohen. All right, I'll go back and practice the other steps."

• • •

I use similar comparisons with all my patients. The Snap Out of It technique can be compared to building a house, sewing a dress, baking a cake or planting a garden. To succeed at these things, you need to follow a plan. If you are baking a cake, you *must* cream the butter and sugar together before you add the flour. If you don't, you'll have a disaster.

To have a successful garden, you have to prepare the soil first. If you skip this step, all your work will be in vain. Suppose you haven't prepared the soil, but you dive ahead anyway and plant your tomato seedlings. About a month later the tomato plants are stunted; some have died.

Step 6: Put It Together

The same will happen with the Snap Out of it technique. For a while you'll be able to struggle along with half a plan, but you'll find that you will be stunted in reaching your goal. And most people will eventually give up when they don't see things happening fast enough. If the tomato plants are withered, you have only two choices:

- You can forget them and walk away from them.

- You can start over—pull them up and replant, following the correct steps this time.

I encourage you to start again at the beginning of this book if you find you haven't followed the steps in the Snap Out of It technique. I encourage you to honestly try the plan as it is described.

• • •

Don't get discouraged. If you're baking a cake you might be dissuaded from even attempting a specific dessert if the recipe goes on for pages and involves many complicated steps. You might think, "I don't have the time." Or you might consider trying the recipe, but then decide against it. You'd reason, "If I spend all that time making the dessert and then it doesn't turn out to be great, I will have wasted all the extra time it takes to make it."

With the Snap Out of It technique you'll find the recipe for success to be short and simple. I can also guarantee that the result of practicing the technique—changing your life—will be the sweet taste of success. There's no need to worry about the recipe being too long and complicated or the results not meeting expectations.

• • •

Jason is an example of someone who was having trouble with the plan and stuck to it. He was using the plan to help him get over the fear of going to Little League baseball. I had given him the band to help him conquer his nervousness.

One day Jason admitted that he had forgotten to practice the Snap Out of It steps for the last four days. He said that he had been wearing the band, but that he had failed to think, "Stop!" and relax.

Then he surprised me by saying, "But I don't feel bad about skipping four days. I'll start again today."

Step 6: Put It Together

"Hey, there's an upbeat attitude." I said. "You know, some people would just give up trying after they missed four days. What makes you convinced you should try again?"

"I don't know exactly, but I do know that it's a little like my baseball game. You see even the big stars strike out, but they don't quit. And then the next time they're up at bat, who knows, sometimes they hit a home run," he explained.

"That's a very positive attitude to have, Jason. It's exactly the type of mind set I'm hoping people will learn with Step 5, Positive Self-Talk." I said. "If you have a few setbacks and you don't reach your goal immediately, it's important that you don't blame yourself. Beating up on yourself will only lead to guilt and depression, which will often result in the return of bad behavior. An attitude that says, 'What's the use in trying—I'm a failure,' will ultimately lead to failure."

He nodded, "When you're up at the plate you've got to think, 'I'm going to hit a home run.' If you think 'I'm going to strike out,' you probably will strike out."

"I'm very happy you're going to start practicing the technique again. Are there any steps you don't understand? What about relaxing? Are you remembering to breath deeply and stretch after you snap the band and say, 'Stop!'?"

Snap Out of It!

It turns out that Jason was leaving out Step 3, Relaxation. This is often the most common step people skip. People leave out this step for a variety of reasons: they don't have the time, they are in a public place, or they don't think it's necessary. Though all the steps are equally important, it's particularly rewarding that you master Step 3. As I explained in Chapter Four, learning to relax as part of the Snap Out of It technique will have a positive effect on all aspects of your life. You will be able to meet all stressful situations armed with relaxation skills.

Watch for Small Improvements

If you find yourself having difficulty changing old ways of thinking and behaving for new ones, remember that it takes time. Don't give up, and keep yourself motivated by watching for small improvements. Looking for improvements has several advantages:

1. Realizing that you have had some success even if it is small will encourage you to keep up the progress towards change.

2. Noticing improvement will stimulate a positive mind set that will influence your success at relaxing and positive self-talk. In short, you'll feel good about yourself.

Be Patient with Yourself

It's not all lost if you don't always succeed. If you are having particular trouble with continually using the Snap Out of It technique to reach your goal, remember to be patient and watch for those small improvements, and give yourself a "pep" talk.

Use Positive Self-Talk

I want you to use positive self-talk not only as a part of Step 5, but also in support of Step 6, Putting It All Together. As you practice the complete six steps encourage yourself. If you treat yourself like a failure when you skip a step, I guarantee you that you will quit trying. This is why many people fail to make a change or meet a goal. They are too hard on themselves when they slip up. Don't fall into this trap.

Go slowly at first.

Did you remember to apply the technique in at least one stressful situation today? Tomorrow aim for two, and the next day promise yourself you'll use the technique a minimum of three times. This approach really works for many people. Try it if you need some tangible way to measure your progress in mastering the six steps.

Today: Use all six steps at once.

Tomorrow: Use the technique twice

The Day after Tomorrow: Your goal is three times.

The Next Day: Go for four, etc.

Ultimately, you won't be counting. You'll move naturally into the technique whenever you need to correct yourself.

Step 6: Put It Together

Rely on your band.

The band is essential to your success. Here are the reasons you need to keep the band on your wrist to meet your goal.

1. The band will remind you that you have made a deliberate decision to change your life.

2. The band is there for you in stressful situations to keep you focused on maintaining your goal.

3. The band will reinforce the steps in the Snap Out of It Technique by helping you to remember to Snap, Stop, Relax, Self-Talk.

● ● ●

Remember:

1. Other people have successfully learned this technique.

2. You may fall down in the beginning.

3. Give yourself some positive feedback and rewards.

Snap Out of It!

4. Watch for small improvements.

5. Remind yourself that though this new skill takes time now, that it will become as automatic as driving a car. Be patient with yourself.

6. Remind yourself why you have learned the technique—to make a very important change in your life.

Your Journal

Treat yourself to a new notebook or blank book that you can use as an ongoing journal. Use this book to write down your continuing success at achieving your goal. For instance jot down the days, weeks, months you have continued to keep meeting your goal. Each day is a success and an investment in your future. Give yourself some accolades.

CHAPTER TEN
Maintenance

Congratulations! You have achieved your goal. Now is the time to celebrate. Take time to evaluate what you have achieved. No matter how small or large your change, you have made an important step. Give yourself a present of some sort—go to a movie, or get a new haircut.

Enjoy your success. Attaining a goal that makes a change in your life is always a significant accomplishment. It takes perseverance and commitment. Reaching your goal, even by using the Snap Out of It technique, took determination. Be proud of all the work and hope you put into your effort to change.

It is very important that you hold on to the six-step process that you invested so much of yourself in learning. In order to make everything that you have acquired yours forever, I'd like to share with you what psychotherapists have known for years.

Snap Out of It!

First, you need to reinforce what you have been doing. That old adage, success breeds success, comes to mind. The more you practice your new found skills, the easier they become. I recommend that you use self- talk, praising yourself to ingrain in your memory the good feelings associated with your achievements.

Second, I recommend that you wear the band at least once a week in order to remind yourself of what you have accomplished. At the same time it gives you an opportunity to consider new goals.

Think of this as maintaining what you've learned. An excellent musician practices daily. This allows her not only to maintain her skills, but to continuously improve and grow. You will find that as you repeatedly follow your routine, the notes you play in your life will be in harmony with change and well-being.

• • •

Some people feel so comfortable using the Snap Out of It technique that as soon as they have met their first challenges, they are eager to start working on yet another goal. They feel like they are "on a roll."

Snap Out of It!

Ted was so elated by his success with controlling his angry outbursts that he felt ready to tackle a new goal-one he never dreamed he could achieve. Armed with his new found confidence and the Snap Out of It approach, he announced that he was going to take on his fear of flying. He was so confident that he would conquer his fear that he booked a flight to Italy.

• • •

Life is a continuing growth experience, ever-changing and expanding. As new goals arise, simply "plug in" the six- step process. You'll find that the transition to the new goal is not that difficult. Success can become enjoyable! It's wonderful to have a sense of control over your habits and actions.

If you feel content for now, there's no need to look for new goals. Enjoy the happiness you've found in meeting your current goal.

"I'm just so happy that I've stopped smoking, I want to be sure I don't slip back," noted Amanda. "Maybe six months from now, I'll think about a new goal to reach."

It's fine to feel this way. It's important to be very protective of your hard-earned success.

Snap Out of It!

What If I Slip?

If, by chance, you slip backwards:

1. Immediately remind yourself of your success in achieving your goal or goals.

2. Start to wear the Snap Out of It band that same day.

3. Put the 6-step Snap Out of It Technique into use with the band.

4. Remind yourself that you're not perfect. It's okay to start again.

Janet came in to see me because she had started worrying about her children again. As before, she was not only making herself unhappy but disturbing her sons with her constant concerns. I asked Janet if she was still practicing the Snap Out of It technique.

She admitted that she wasn't. "I'm too busy," was one of the excuses she gave.

Snap Out of It!

"It's actually easier to do the Snap Out of It technique than it is to spend time ruminating about all the things that might happen to Rob and Joe," was my first comment.

Janet agreed and we explored why she had so many reasons not to use the program.

• • •

If you find that you are repeatedly coming up with the same reasons (excuses) for allowing yourself to slip back, ask yourself:

1. What thoughts do I have about changing my behavior?

2. How are these detrimental?

3. Can I make these into positive ones so that I can continue to make progress?

Janet found that worrying made her feel important. She could be the martyr; she was the person who cared so much about everyone that she took all future imaginary crises on her shoulders. Of course, this was not the case. It was, as Dr.

Snap Out of It!

Ellis would say , irrational thinking.

Janet was able to get in touch with this thinking , restructure it, and get back to the plan. If you're having trouble staying on track, you may also be attached to your symptom. Like Janet, explore what may be in your path and rewrite the tape.

YOUR VISION

This book has been an attempt to dramatically alter your attitudes and to change your negative behavior into positive action. It's a relearning process—one which helps us prevail over our early shaping.

One of the reasons it works is because it gives you the freedom to make choices. When you are in the grip of old self-defeating messages that are automatic, you don't even know they are there. You're just reacting to a way in which you've been programmed.

Now you can relax and replace those old negative thoughts with uplifting positive ones. You have empowered yourself. No more victim mentality. Think about how you used to be. Ask yourself, "How am I now?"

Snap Out of It!

- Close your eyes and picture yourself in this new role.

- Think about the goal you've tackled.

- See yourself in the path you took to reach this goal.

- Feel the warm feelings that relaxing and taking control can promote.

- See yourself now as you've always wanted to be.

Anyone can acquire this technique. It just requires a belief in the process and overcoming initial resistance to make a "new" you. Don't just imagine your vision, live it.

• • •

This brings me back to the goal of writing the book. I have invited you to approach change in a new step-by-step way. It will help you to discover a freeing up and a clarity of thought that will be yours forever.

BIBLIOGRAPHY

Amen, D. G. *Change Your Brain, Change Your Life*. New York: Times Books, 1998.

————. *Don't Shoot Yourself in the Foot*. New York: Warner Books, 1992.

Bain, J. A. *Thought Control in Everyday Life*. New York: Funk and Wagnalls, 1928.

Benson, H. and Baim, M. "Mind /Body Medicine: Clinical Perspectives and Update, Harvard Medical School," Department of Continuing Education, Longboat Key Florida, February 22–26, 1999.

Cautela, J. and Wisocki, P. "The Thought Stopping Procedure: Description, Application, and Learning Theory Interpretations," *The Psychological Record*, 1977,Winter: Vol. 27 (1): 255–264.

Ellis, A. *Reason and Emotion in Psychotherapy*. New York: Stuart, 1962.

Snap Out of It!

Foa, E. B. and Rothbaum, B. O. *Treating the Trauma of Rape: Cognitive-Behavioral Therapy for PTSD*. New York: The Guilford Press, 1998.

George, M. S. , Ketter, T. A. , Parekh, P. I. ,Horowitz, B. , et. al. "Brain activity during transient sadness and happiness in healthy women." *American Journal of Psychiatry*, 1955 Mar: Vol. 152 (3): 341–351.

McKay, M. , Davis, M. and Fanning, P. *Thoughts and Feelings: The Art of Cognitive Stress Intervention*. Oakland, California: New Harbinger Publications, 1981.

Wolpe, J. *The Practice of Behavior Therapy*. New York: Pergamon Press, 1969.